SOME WILD GYPSY

by

BRENDA FLEET

To Richard

Something I wrote when I was still 'flower child'. May you enjoy some of it.

Brenda

9.10.85

Borealis Press
Ottawa, Canada
1976

Copyright ©Borealis Press, 1976

All rights reserved

ISBN 0-919594-52-2

Published with assistance of the
Ontario Arts Council

Cover photograph by R. Manicom

The Borealis Press Limited
9 Ashburn Drive
Ottawa, Canada, K2E 6N4

Printed and bound in Canada

Some Wild Gypsy

BRENDA FLEET

ACKNOWLEDGEMENTS

I wish to thank Michel Saikali and Danielle Levasseur for reading the manuscript and giving me a critical perspective on the Québecois situation.

I wish to thank Sharon Rusu for her assistance in the final arrangement of this manuscript and for providing an introduction at the beginning of this book.

Some of the poems which are included here have appeared, though in often different form, in my previous publications and are reprinted through kind permission of Fiddlehead Poetry Books. They include:

Catching the Sun's Fire
Bullets and Cathedrals
Sullen Earth.

The poem "Twilight: at Glasgow" has already appeared under the title "Glasgow Twilight" in the anthology, **Poets of the Capital**, Borealis Press.

I wish to thank R. Manicom for the cover photography and the black and white portrait.

And all those who urged me to carry it on.

INTRODUCTION

Through her role as "Earth Mother mating the sensual with the abstract", Brenda Fleet instills life and breath into her creation of **Some Wild Gypsy.**

As a poet, whose personal task is admittedly complex and, at times, overwhelming, Fleet captures her own personal emotions and perceptions, vibrant and alive, and transforms them intact in her poetry. She perceives with vividness and honesty the constant flux, ambiguity and moments of luminosity in her world. Her perceptions result in images which are as disparate as a perfectly molded church steeple and a "witch" with her "deck of Tarot". In her book **Some Wild Gypsy**, Fleet becomes the joiner of opposites as her poetry strives to move beyond dualities, beyond the "ferociously circular" toward her personal artistic ideal . . . "Becoming".

The structure of **Some Wild Gypsy** is in four select sections each illustrative of part of an evolutionary process toward self-completion. The four sections however must be examined as a whole, a continuum, ever-evolving from one psychic, social and artistic state to another. Beginning with **The Romantic Voice** one notes the author's innocence of perception and the almost child-like recollections of a city whose "naiveté astounds" almost as though it were her own innocence that was so astounding. This section shelters the voice of history, of a past that has somehow become inexplicably bound up with a future that is yet unknown. Here is the infant voice of the gypsy, with his expectations, hope and a "will to survive all hell". Yet, here too is expressed the author's sadness at the dawning realization of the multifarious aspects of an often cruel world, of a present that shares no compassionate link with the past.

The second section, **The Ironic Voice,** effectively undercuts the first. Gone is the innocence and in its place a cool, cutting intellectual tone is presented. The poems of this section exemplify Fleet's finely-honed creative abilities as she critically evaluates the despair which results from a loss of innocence. From **Elegy for the Turn of the Century** through the short story **Intrusions,** Fleet cuts through the crass capacity of our everyday lives laying bare the workings of her own inner psyche, trembling and unsure, searching for some sense of personal identity. **The Ironic Voice** ends in ambiguity.

The intellectual derision and self-seeking tone of **The Ironic Voice** gives way to the almost humble, self-accepting poetry of **The Voice of the Lover.** This section portrays a conscious movement on the part of the author beyond the romanticized flights of fantasy of the first section and the cryptic, highly stylized poems of the second. Here lies the beginning of the voice of self-appraisal. The poems of this section exude a greater understanding and even acceptance of human frailties. The mocking tone of the former section evolves to a gradual awareness of the power that exists in "love as the greatest form of right attention", the spiritual as opposed to the emotional and purely intellectual.

The last section, **The Voice of the Absurd,** finalizes the author's movement from childhood to maturity. The poems of this section appear as the fruits of the voice of self-appraisal which had its beginning in the former section. The poem **Wheel of Fortune** probably best reveals the author's feelings about her confrontation with a reality which has offered more pain than happiness, more grief than laughter. The voyage to the inner self has ended. Fleet has discarded the psychic and social encrustations of a hostile existence in order to free, at last, the final voice of the gypsy.

Sharon Rusu

Some Wild Gypsy

Brenda Fleet

CONTENTS

Page

Dedication	xii
Quotation	xiii
Preface	xiv

1. The Romantic Voice 1
The First Wild Gypsy: A Legend 3
Grandfather 8
Heritage of Quebec: Elegy I 9
Heritage of Quebec: Elegy II 13
Heritage of Quebec: Elegy III 15
I am the Tourist 18

2. The Ironic Voice 19
Elegy for the Turn of the Century 21
Twilight: at Glasgow 23
I Left You 24
Let Them Find Out 26
Gypsy's Apology 27
Dilemma 28
By Way of Explanation 29
The All-Nighter 30
To the Pole-Vaulter 31
Notes, 1968 32
Notes, 1975 33
Oriental Cup 34
Lightly 35
Candles for Prisons 36
Prisons I 37
Prisons II 38
Prisons III 39
Prisons IV 40
The Other I 41
The Other II 42

CONTENTS

Page

Trio 43
Off the Hook 44
Undone 45
Intrusions: A Story 46
3. The Voice of the Lover 53
For his Father's son 55
Clay 57
Taking Leave 58
Your Heart 59
Absence I 60
Absence II 61
Gypsy's Reappraisal 62
Bittersweet 63
His Gift 64
My Gift 65
Stars 66
Rerouted 67
Requiem for Prisons I 68
Requiem for Prisons II 69
Requiem for Prisons III 70
Requiem for Prisons IV 71
Requiem for Prisons V 72
4. The Voice of the Absurd 73
Voyages 75
The River 78
Elegy 80
Unmarked: At Lauterbrunnen 81
You're in Again 82
You Return 84
Bonnie & Clyde 85

CONTENTS

Page

Michael I 86
Michael II: For the Time Being 88
Michael III: Susie, died 1975 90
Wheel of Fortune 92
Sanitorium 93
Alchemy I 94
Alchemy II 95
Longing 96

Autobiographical Notes 97

Dedication
To Fred Cogswell

"It has always been easier to fake happiness and shut up about the fakery than to tell the truth and expose the myth that caused the disillusion — even at the expense of perpetrating the myth for others."

Scoring
by Dan Greenburg

PREFACE

. . . What was inward is turned outward, what was a merely fluid subjective state becomes cystallized, made objective. The experience ceases to exist only for myself, and takes on life for others as a moment in the whole poetic process – the experience in poetic form is no longer mine.

This means, in terms of poetic criticism, that my analysis of my own poem becomes as valid or as invalid as anyone else's analysis. As poet I am afforded a special glimpse into lived experience, but no special insights into the meaning of that poem. A poem stands on its own two feet and breathes with its own breath.

I am poet, not critic. Let the critics decide merit in terms of the historical poetic process, in terms of imagery, psychology, sociology – whatever external discipline they wish to impose upon poetry or whatever internal discipline they wish to derive from it.

I am concerned with building something strong, living, independent of me. I am an Earth Mother mating the sensual with the abstract: just as my fingers grow downwards like roots they reach upwards to the sky. The superb mating of the purely immediate sensual life with the supra – or metaphysical being of language gives birth to the most paradoxical creature ever flung from its mother's loins–the poem.

1. THE ROMANTIC VOICE

THE FIRST WILD GYPSY:
A LEGEND

Once upon a time in the time of our great-grandfathers when ships still sailed across the sea to the gulf of the St. Lawrence and docked at Quebec City, a royal ship from Spain with full sails bore not only silks and perfumes from its aristocracy, but also some of its embarrassing illegitimate offspring.

One of these was a dark baby boy with still darker lashes and a will to survive all hell.

After the ship had bartered its stock for new supplies from the New Land, and sailed fading and folding its white wings towards what was, no doubt, a burst of orange sunset, they found him in torn clothes lying between the great rocks and fish nets at low tide. And they named him no name at all. For he was the first wild gypsy, and they were poor French folk who couldn't afford to take him in; but the mother and father had far too great compassion and charity to leave him. So he did not die, although some famous Spanish count with a gold belt and his stocky willing mistress never knew.

The boy grew up unaware of his ancestry, laughing out loud with his family of brothers and sisters, some of whom died in infancy, others, later, of tuberculosis or malnutrition, but he of the strong brown shoulders borne by the sea did not die. He ate potato pie and blood pudding around a long wood table, though occasionally the size of the meals shrank noticeably, as did the size of the family when one or another half-sibling was quietly buried and one less plate was put on the table and no one laughed at all.

My great-grandfather finally adopted the family name that once meant "the tiny green of spring". Names were one with the fruit of the earth; and the people stood in awe of the first luminous leaves standing out bravely on a small tree, leaves of light, stronger than the Quebec winters.

He married into common French stock. He chose well, with an intuitive grasp of survival. From him there came many children and grandchildren for his seed was fruitful and his descendants multiplied upon the shores of the St. Lawrence and the ancient city of Quebec, although it was now a city besieged and held by a people who did not speak his language.

His one daughter, my grandmother, inherited the salt water fierceness and the unwillingness to give up in the face of poverty. She of the sea waters and the first spring leaf stood resilient and unvanquished. She had many sons and daughters, several distinctly Spanish, and among her own people her ancestry was questioned for her cheekbones were too high and regal, her daughters too beautiful and fine-boned, to boast of pure French peasant blood.

They endured. When the Americans first came and made of the land a place to be a tourist, and my grandmother had not a cent to her name but many fine daughters, there were ways and means to put bread on the table. She of the strong shoulders baked many a potato pie and moved when she could no longer pay the rent. Then at last when the domination of the Americans on the English Canadians created many more tourist attractions, my grandmother swallowed her gypsy pride to become the pastry cook on the small pleasure boat that cruised up and down the Saguenay for ladies in white gowns and English-speaking gentlemen with gloves and staw hats.

She had inherited from her father, the first gypsy, that same urge for the sea and wept when the pleasure boat went too far inland, breaking her blood ties with the tides. In the legend's story as it was passed down to me, she wept also at being unable to multiply her pastry ingredients so as to bake for one hundred at one time, and so she stayed up all night baking for ten and ten and ten until her contract was fulfilled. The debt paid, she walked nobly with clear eyes from the pleasure boat back to the soil of Quebec, leaving behind so much false laughter, champagne, and small white cupcakes with cherries and ladies' fingers.

There was a timeless time in Quebec when the winters were much longer, the winds howling over the cliff from the river, and the snowbanks much higher than ladies and gentlemen, most of whom stayed indoors anyhow, leaving the beautiful dark streets with cystalline snow to the poor, the derelicts, wanderers and sometime lovers.

Long ago on a well-known street in Quebec my grandmother's husband, who kept a mistress and did not have very much money, went to the most compassionate of his daughters (falling back on the gypsy resilience whose blood did not course in his veins) to confess. His mistress was with child, and the legend has it that it was Christmas eve and he had no place to bring her. He needed ten dollars, a very large sum in Quebec in those long ago days, begging it from his gypsy daughter who with sullen pride gave it to him. She accompanied him down the streets abandoned to the poor on winter nights, to bring his mistress with child to a Catholic home. As the three of them walked like beggars over the immense snowbanks, one guilty, one in the pain of Eve, one young and proud, the woman with her huge belly suddenly cried out.

There in the simplicity which is birth she lay on the snowbanks and brought her child into the world. My grandfather wrapped him in his old scarf and took him to an orphanage. The mistress got up (for she yet possessed the untamed French will) and returned home. The daughter wept and went back to her mother, saying nothing. All this happened in the short span of a few hours on a Quebec night. And the daughter who was the compassionate one became my mother.

My grandmother, my mother and I spoke French together. I learned to say the rosary, tasted hot potato pie, saw three blue eggs abandoned in a nest near the country house, picked strawberries (giving away only those that were green and keeping the red glistening ones in my pocket), and never wandered into the luring swamp of the extraordinary white flowers.

The legend which is my childhood has it that I was lured by something else, the lure of dangerous water, a flooded dam after a heavy rain, bringing back the ancient gypsy heritage, the taste for high tides and the sea. But I did not drown. I also endured.

My grandmother of the spring leaf and strong back did not so endure. Many times the Spanish blood brought her back to life, and the doctors said she was a woman who did not want to die. She told us all to die fighting. And if ever she found a way to come back to the earth she would force her way, breaking down the doors.

I was only five but I understood, being in direct line of fiery ancestry and undefeated blood. But the loss of my grandmother was my first crucial loss, superceded only by another, much later, from another legend, a wild gypsy himself whose ancestry is as dubious and beautiful as were his promises.

After my grandmother's death, everything changed, even the city, and I was to learn a foreign language and a new religion at the bidding of my English father. That was the time of ugly rumours among my family, that I had turned my back to join league with those who stood as white English conquerors. That was the time of English schools and the end of many French words. In the schools my English grammar was never perfect enough, my accent still ridiculous, my aptitude for English comfort still too low.

Today at Rideau Hall in Ottawa which speaks of quiet British custom and tidy manners, and not at all of potato pie or fish nets or rosaries, a governor-general who presents literary awards to French and English Canadian writers is denounced by those from my city, Quebec. He is a quiet man. I do not fully understand the cries that come from my own French people; I cannot fully understand their anger as they call down "the repressive forces of the power hierarchy working against the body, desires, and dreams" of Quebecers. I believe it must have something to do with my legend, my grandmother sweating on the Saguenay cruise; but I no longer know.

My anger is not accepted as valid from those same people who are my flesh and blood. My anger speaks in an English vocabulary and has learned to wear fashionable garden hats at Rideau Hall. My anger is mixed with empathy for those who do not even comprehend the nature of the violence which they now see exploding before them. My anger blossoms out in words that speak the genteel and quiet English which my French people detest. My father's people do not accept my sympathy, too easily mistaken for condescension, especially from a half-breed whom they have so well educated, whom they see faltering during the propriety of introductions and the lifting of a tea-cup.

My Quebec identity is ravaged and torn. I have no identity, I am part of an old legend, it was I who came from the sea in the time of my great-grandfather, and it is for my dilemma that my split cultural family curses and spits. For me they close their angry hearts but for me, also, open their arms to the gypsy infant on the ragged shore.

And a time will come when we shall all be the first wild gypsies.

May 22, 1975

GRANDFATHER

1.

Grandfather gone to a home somewhere
face of eighty-eight that knows more than tells
you lost both your wives and talk to no-one

2.

My family tells me they visit sometimes
they wondered why, the last time, you'd taken
your chair from the window to sit facing the wall

HERITAGE OF QUEBEC: ELEGY I

1.

My city, my old terraces,
with the few cobble roads that remain,
the men that work and sweat at your ferry,
why have you remained so inarticulate
why so impassive? The clash of traffic
defiles you; you have forgotten your past;
and still you turn to me
for a song of faithfulness.

Take a good look at yourself first!
What do you know of the rest of the world?
Your naiveté astounds me!
History has rushed past you,
and you toy with your blank thoughts
as if you were toothless and senile
taking your pleasure from the fraying
churches and towers that are left
smiling at the riverbank, decaying . . .

A slave who knows nothing
a slave without pride
offering little resistance
to "progress", to "modernization" —

What do you know of pavement or of machines?
What of the miles of neon lights
the sprawling centres "for sales and bargains"
that lie in wait
for your slow death?

No, it is useless,
your self-knowing spirit has never dawned,
it is too late now
your thighs are too old to remember your conquests;
how can I glorify you in the poetry meant only for heroes
now that you are debauched
it is hardly necessary for me to remain faithful!

2.

Still, like the crazy lover that I am,
the old memories of our young nights
seduce my heart's rancour.
My family lived here,
and my mother's family
the past lives in the hearts of old people . . .

My grandmother who died from exhaustion
stealing a life for herself from poverty
could neither read nor write, but sang
the old songs to the gas-lamps, and as a child
I sniffed the sharp smell of kerosene,
mixed with the plaintive songs . . .
They were poor, they did what they could
in the basse ville, my grandmother
sent out her prettiest daughters
to the butcher for meat.
"Do what you can" – the whispered password –
and can there be any sin when

children are starving? "Do what you can" —
but button your blouses if you meet the priest.

My mother's brother, at the age of thirteen,
died from tuberculosis or goiter;
he wanted to be a saint — they had to stop him
from sleeping on a bed of nails he had built.
After his death, the priests voted in favour
of his canonization. My grandmother preferred
obscurity . . .

Another uncle has recently died;
in his youth, he was an artist,
he had hope and ambition; a sculpture of his
won a first prize in New York (far horizon)
he studied aux Beaux-Arts until he got married
then his wife insisted on a better life;
he sold his paintbox for china plates
and ended his life as a postman

My mother's sister was schooled for a month
in a convent, though her eyes were resentful
the sex-urge dominant
at night, she'd escape for better places
and the nuns found her habit in the chapel
tucked behind the organ

My aunts are unhappily married
there is no priest in the family
only one uncle remains

3.

Tell me in your turn, my half-brothers
how splendid the view of the Château looks
from the torn-down houses of the docks
tell me of the magnificent porcelain up there
the lights that glitter like jewels
you see them as you look up through the laundry
that your wives hang on the clothes-lines
Explain the disparity to me
do not forget your past

St-Jean le Baptiste passes
in slow, ornate procession
along the old streets of Quebec
especially in summer
the priests wear their robes
the American tourists
ride the calèches
your sacred images
are in the hands of moneymakers
and at this you cannot be passive

O my mother, my mother
in all this
in my city that is whore to the tourists
in my city where they sell the old people's
rocking-chairs and crosses,
remind me of the past
resurrect the old bitterness
what else do the old people conceal
behind their ancient
resignation?

HERITAGE OF QUEBEC:
ELEGY II

Inside the slow dream
of centuries, I never cried
my complaint. I am a rumour
in the hearts of my people, in their arms
carefully folded over their skirts
in their stance, placid as farmers' wives
watching the fields, in their hands
corroded by clutching the crucifix
in mute prayers, rosaries without speech.

I am the vegetable woman with a Pepsi sign
I am eleven apples at trente à la douzaine
I have learned to keep my eyes closed

In scattered towns the high steeple
frowns in the evening with its long shadow
while uncles are paying little girls for kisses
and women are walking the streets well
and all are forgiven in Sunday's ignorance
I am the vague hurt in the girl's eyes
and calculation covered by lipstick
the melancholy of old men
who gamble on chance erections

I am a people twisted from the soil

In my one city Quebec I am sold as a charm
that ladies' jewellers place upon bracelets
in so many sizes, I am a cross,
a saint, a Château Frontenac, a maple leaf

in the tired summer of shop-girls and clerks
I speak a broken English to broken English
and note in my accounts the American money
and order more relics of the saint that sold best

In the slow dream of centuries
J'vas m'eduquer moé, tu vas voér maudit
inside the sleeping potion
la kâlisse d'église de marde, passe moé ton lighter
moving inaudibly through time
penses-tu qui vont m'avoér Jésus Marie
The slow murmur of twisted roots
the bent tree watching its twisted shadow

J'ai beaucoup d'éspoir, rien ne m'arrêtera
Je cueille des mots pour vous chanter ma peine
un jour vous entendrez le cri de ma douleur

Out of the slow dream of centuries
I lifted my voice
once, and cried for blood

HERITAGE OF QUEBEC:
ELEGY III

          1.

winter solstice goes from us
    unwillingly,
winds howl over frozen lake
blizzard-dust covers branches
    colourless,
save for some russet twigs;
a road covered by snow-banks
    goes nowhere

young man at the window
    snow-blurred,
watches the wind from the lake
howling, tenacious, its claws
    in his soul;
the surrender of frost
to his hard breathing,
    his single vision

dismal February, swept bare,
    but fire-glow
shines on a mother's wild hair,
memories remain in her arms
    of a child
once soothed into milk and dreams;
but leans, today, at the cage-bars
    fists against storm

2.

He has opened the door
and left his home,
consciousness strained
to the breaking-point

The coarse simplicity
of a stricken tree
has broken the tedium
of a hundred years

Mother, be still,
return to your rocking-chair
create a new requiem
for your son's new age

3.

An ideology is born, wind-swept,
from that October violence; winter
rages, unrelieved, fully conscious;
the priests are struck dumb, confess
themselves, their ancient failings.

Not the spring's drunkenness
drives out the young man; not
the sweet leaf, the spring rain.
This winter harshness is forever
in his brain, his young limbs.

4.

The moon tonight is wild with
barren hills, and clouds break over
her face, oppose the full light,
pale glinting; a night made
desolate by countless farewells.

And far he goes, with his mark
that others like him will acknowledge;
from village to village his bitterness
corrodes his mouth, hands, limbs:
memories of a country's decadence.

5.

Old men watch the calendars,
wait for the foul year to pass;
mothers by the fireside mutter
vague prayers from a past age.

A young man spits out false hope,
his mouthful of poisoned berries.

I AM THE TOURIST
to Kim and Ted

With both of you gripping your magic markers
retracing desire on the European map
Kim holding the baby high in the streets
in the crowds in the demonstrations

I am the tourist who never joined up;
I missed the action to visit the ruins.

Remember the undergraduate ideals
when the pill was the only revolution
in the '60's we swore to be free
and saw the '50's and fraternities topple

I am the tourist who perused your concerns;
I avoided the action and joined with the ruins.

Forgive me for leaving the marches behind
while you prepared for the front
I didn't even protest the war measures act
though some policeman arrested an artist
for possession of books on Cubism

Your friend, a federal public servant
remembers her Québecois cousins at coffee
and tries to forget a life-long illness.
So return to your wars, and I'll stay with mine
I promise, when I've healed my heart,
we'll trade postcards on respective victories.

2. THE IRONIC VOICE

ELEGY FOR THE TURN OF THE CENTURY

1.

You left three sons
who wept when you died
and a hole in the universe
not even a hole full of maggots
but a void, silver and embossed
like a vanished threat

2.

Old lady, you left behind
an aristocracy gone at the guts
eaten by pigeons and barristers
too fine for the neon of streets
unsuitable for pizzerias
not even a catch-phrase commercial
could give it life, a grunt and a groan
it is too private a name, it will die

3.

And in the rooms still veiled
with your discreet touches
with centuries of polite society
lingering with the care of an engraver
upon the flaws of the intruder
there with your only art
you may be glimpsed
poised in blue and silver
waiting at the evening's window

for your expectations to be met
for your will
to be acknowledged

                4.

O lady
you really held on
you must have known they were gone
your body and your world
how you clung to both
how they slipped from your grasp
the one, obscene as any flesh
the other, not even going out in style

TWILIGHT: AT GLASGOW

sadness in little bundles
collects even in the corners
of children's morning-games

twilight hardly descends
over the smokestacks, the flat brick
of still-echoing exits

now vanish the rehearsals
of first communion, the black nun
with strict hands

now the lady of the evening
about to receive white-throated guests
stands at her threshold

not even her glances toward
the pink evening conceal
the faint agony at her mouth

I LEFT YOU
>Written for a Teachers' Conference
at McGill University, August '71

I left you to rid us both
of bitterness, to seek instruction
elsewhere than in classrooms
empty with my own words;
while you stayed on, thrust on
by eventual movement of grade
upon grade, though the same eyes
looked on from faces endlessly
the same: indifferent, hostile,
or eager, the "challenge" of
your profession, a self-chosen
martyrdom, unworthy of glory and
worn-out.
    Let my return be softer
though not without unyielding core;
I sing the same song with you
who advance in eagerness;
the rest may well be offended.

My song praises no facts,
no prohibitions, not the informers
set up as spies upon life,
not these informers' lists, their
records, data, and all other
blackmail. I sing of plain
speech, without lies; of networks
destroyed, and the gift of clear
speech unhindered.

In my didactics I consign
the treacherous and ignorant,
the dull-eyed and forgetful
to twenty-four hours of
indecent nakedness. I strip
you of your clothes and say:

Go to the fields, forests,
quivering fields, that the
Great Breath lift away
your years of paperwork;
let the Great Swell
invade your open mouths;
be instructed in all manner
of chaos and indecency;
let the wind forever
hide your clothes.

Return then, and tear down the concrete,
to let each of your walls be a window.

LET THEM FIND OUT
à Danielle

Let the secretaries whisper
furtively to the clerks,
the shoe-shine boys
the sunshine girls
their coterie of close friends
who have friends closer still

Let them whisper in parks at noon
where flowers will overhear
and happily be nodding,
or in restaurants
where plastic roses
will burst into buds

Let them calculate
how often we make love
how often we can make love;
they will be astounded,
return to their diets
take out their files

Let them find out, dying in envy.
Let the flowers live on
and we shall whisper back:
"Bavardez mes frères,
Bavardez mes frères,
Il en restera toujours quelque chose! "

GYPSY'S APOLOGY

1.

I'm sorry I'm not beautiful:
I'm a witch, they say, with silver teeth
crazily shuffling her deck of Tarot
and turning up the thirteenth card
I'm some wild gypsy playing
havoc in bed, sliding needles
into my sleeping men, a sort of
soft intrusion in their lives.

2.

I'm sorry I'm not beautiful.
Rumours circulate so fast —
first thing the Nikon man's
selling my lover a soft focus lens
(my eyes are of chrome and my skin shines)
and next thing the neighbourhood has the slides
which glow in the dark and turn mad in his hands —
I'm sorry that I am not beautiful.

DILEMMA
To John L.

two men, academics
are seated on a bus
too close to each other

they speak of their research
their visits to England
and do not look at each other

BY WAY OF EXPLANATION

You say you like cats and
cats have always found your lap
cuddly and warm

Well this one's got balls
and knows you've got them too

THE ALL-NIGHTER

The University of Ottawa has
asked for comments or suggestions
following my participation in the
Poetry All-Nighter, October '74.

I didn't write in to ask:
why were all my heroes drunk?
and their fine verse cursing stupidity
read as indifferently as a prayer book?

Monologue followed monologue.
They were all drunk.
Their speech broke into their rhythms.
The noblest among them aspired only

to try pinching my bottom.

TO THE POLE-VAULTER

Irving Layton, I have always
wanted to get past
my make-up your cynicism
my teens your senility
my crotch your restlessness

long enough to say
your writing has soul
and so do you, big toughie

NOTES, 1968

The Editor of *Quarry*, Mr. Barbour, has written.
He said DEAR CONTRIBUTOR at the top of the slip of paper
WE ARE UNABLE TO USE YOUR CONTRIBUTION
– and at the bottom, has produced small legible notes:

"One of your poems is quite good, it moves well.
However you are not attentive to rhythm.
As a result, the others move too slowly.

"A better performance will result
from the following alterations:

"Remove all articles.
Your 'ands' are unnecessary.
Furthermore, cut at your poems.
They move too slowly.

"Remain in the active voice,
especially with verbs, for concision.
N.B. Use concrete nouns for precision.

"We like some of what you say.
Read Ezra Pound, he may be helpful.

"And try us again in October
when we get a new Editor."

NOTES, 1975
Sonnet to Ian

a
b
b
a

a
b
b
a

c
d
c
d

e
e

ORIENTAL CUP

Its dangerous dragons, white
on the green contours, roar
at the golden handle.

Ferociously circular:
monsters tamed in china.

LIGHTLY

Come enter my world,
step lightly. You will listen
to my violent songs, you will
enter my abyss.

Disclose yourself gently
as only trees know, when
their leaves glisten
blissful with growing.

Enter my strange, my foreign
boundaries. Love. Though I
show you dangers, as of
ice threatening spring.

CANDLES FOR PRISONS

No ordinary gift: its implications
disturbing and well-chosen.

Candlesticks that came without a word from you,
except that someone else explained they were antique.

They may have lit prisons: upright black chains,
stiffened to stand from the base,

posture unreasonable, crowned by two candles,
not new, but burnt almost to the bottom,

though never lit by me. This is your gift:
these orange candles sitting on stiffened chains.

Eccentric and doomed as any love from you.

PRISONS I

in the safety of
reflected things, I
hide, seek refuge:

the mirrored face,
mute; the indirect
sunlight on windows

things caught from
too violent bursting
on the self's fragility —

then held, imprisoned

PRISONS II

"I didn't call you when in Ottawa
having no inclination for human contact."
You wandered around stores,
watched people, felt disinclined

You couldn't have guessed
I'd been lost for over a week
holding on to my stuffed animals
somewhere between sleep and pain
wondering how to reach you

My war, you understand,
was very delicate.
Had you called, you might have
saved the pink lion from death,
from netted gladiators

PRISONS III

"I am entrusting
you
with this fragile, torn-apart
self."

The reply:

"I
am not
your friend."

PRISONS IV

I'm a little glass doll: hold me.

Hold me up to your eyes
you'll see the wall through me,
you'll see the door.

Hold me up to a mirror
you'll see yourself.

THE OTHER
I

Is she placid, the other
to whom you are the safety
of duties and household, anger
of daily care, children?

She will not know the pain
you give to me, nor how open-
deep my body in remembering
all that you must disavow.

Another dark day when I
cry openly in front of you
to no avail, while you
advise on how to live alone

THE OTHER
II

She is far closer to you than I am.
She has smiled, and torn
you limb from limb.

She is far safer to be seen with.
She feeds on your half-lies, while
I swallow the truth whole.

She is more dangerous than you think.
Her every movement towards you is
your own past, beckoning.

I have not seen her.
Yet I see her live in each response
you make towards me, blindly.

TRIO

Our pauses will be
long enough
for a child's scream

We will pretend
to ignore this,
from our separate chairs

Between phrases,
you and she
will plot my murder

Or I will be
assassin: kill you both
as you conspire

As simple as a look
shot across the room:
thus we undo the other

OFF THE HOOK

I'm living my
dying days with you.
Cameras won't
tell on you, your film's
gone blank and I
won't tell it, ruin it.

Why not destroy
the evidence: photographs
you never let me take,
your backhand signature,
love on a carbon copy.

There's more to it than
anyone knows and I
haven't a mouth or toes
and can't spring up or
leap out of the bag.

The brown paper bag —
don't worry, it fits;
I wear it around and look
out though slits. I've
absent-mindedly lost
your number, the ring
I'm sealed like a package
and don't know a thing

If I'm ever let out
I swear I won't look.
Go ahead, try to ring true.
The phone's off the hook
dear, and so are you.

UNDONE

Caressing
my long hair
your fingers
vibrate with hatred

I may as well be
stretched out flat,
feeding the acid nodes
of EEG machines,
and how they press
metallic fingernails
into the skull

Knowing you so well,
I spell out on white paper
the shared data of rage
I understand the
violently undone,
those, irretrievable

INTRUSIONS:
A STORY

She felt a certain uneasiness in the air as she gazed out of the kitchen window. The flowers, planted earlier that spring, were in bloom; the fountain in the pool invaded the stillness. Her husband, Thomas, was clipping the hedges; and the regular clip-clip, faintly heard, added monotony to the summer day.

Evelyn poured herself some tea and sat down. She was so tired, and she searched to remember exactly what great feat, what task, could have tired her so. Her mind was empty, except for the vague knowledge that she had been married for twenty years. She supposed that she should not complain. The house, after all, was theirs; they had a car, even if they had no children; Thomas provided well. She should not complain – but what weariness, what uneasiness, as she lifted the cup to her lips and listened to the steady clipping of hedges.

Thomas had built the house himself. He had ushered his bride into his lovely country home, only five miles from town. Besides his office work, which he did scrupulously, he tended to the general upkeep of his architectural creation with devotion. He sang in his bath every morning, and liked his eggs well-done. On Saturdays, he had a morning swim in his pool, and preferred a late breakfast, with two cups of coffee instead of one.

Happy at all costs, stubborn and practical, Thomas was seriously considering having his hair dyed to its natural brown. Evelyn had told him he was a fool. But his secretary had thought it a marvellous idea, and in such matters he granted her a more acute critical sense. Of course, nothing had been decided yet; it was an idea, only an idea (he had shouted this to his wife across the table), and there was no use in getting upset over his hair right now.

The sun was a bit warm for four o'clock. Should he put on a hat? The hedges had grown outward another quarter of an inch; the effect was terrible, almost a prophecy of disorder. So, as he hummed quietly to himself, he clipped the branches back to their proper proportions.

Evelyn ruminated over the past, though most of her memories were blurred by the thin veils which time deposits so quietly. Had she ever lived differently? She thought, sometimes, that the fault lay with her, that her own emotions had become anaesthetized. But when and where had this happened? No great catastrophe had murdered her spirit so that, ridden with all sorts of illnesses and strange attacks, her hand trembling slightly as she raised the teacup, she could point to it in triumph and declare: that was it. Exactly this killed me. It happened then . . . No, there was no such cry of exultation. Nothing had ever happened to her at all.

Her revery was abruptly terminated. Thomas slammed the front door and walked over to the table.

"Well, you look cheerful today," she said. All the old bitterness rose in her throat.

"And you, my dear Evelyn, look rather pale. Have you taken your pills yet?"

"No."

"Then take them. What are you waiting for? Do you think I enjoy the thought of seeing you collapse in your chair?"

He went into the dining room and stared out the large windows overlooking the terrace. Everything was still. She could hear him shuffling nervously about.

"I'm going to town for a while, dear, to pick up some papers at the office," he said.

"But it's four o'clock, Thomas, and you know very well that you don't need your papers."

"Well, then, I'm going out. Out. I won't be long. I'll be back by six."

"Oh, I've stopped believing you. Do what you like. I don't care. I'm old and sick. I'm quite content to sit here alone and wait. You're always late, anyhow. And I'm always alone."

It was an old trick, but it always worked. Thomas knew it was true; that she had no friends, no children, nothing to do. She relied on him for everything; he was her strength, her mentor, her possession, and her amusement. How could she help it?

This time Thomas spoke more softly.

"Evelyn, dear, why don't you take your pills and lie out on one of the lawn chairs near the pool. The fresh air will be good for you. I'll look around for some new magazines for you while I'm in town."

"But I've read all the latest."

"Then I'll buy you a new book. There's always something new, isn't there? There's always a new toy to play with. I keep you amused, don't I? I bought you the lawn chairs only last week!"

"I know, Thomas, and you're very kind. I guess I'm just a cranky old thing. You run along to the office, now."

He patted her on the shoulder, pretending to ignore the shudder that passed through her body as his fingers touched her skin. He could feel her tightening, although she knew that there was no question of that any longer. He never asked anything of her. Still the ancient reflex of her body whenever he came near her. He hadn't bought twin beds yet. He still kept up the old pretense. But he knew better than to reach out.

Evelyn sighed nervously.

"Six o'clock, then, be seeing you!" she said, not casually enough. Thomas walked out without saying a word.

She had nothing to look forward to. Through long and empty days, Evelyn had sat near the pool, lost in the tumble of water from the fountain and the chlorinated depths of the pool. The reflections had shimmered like white and green lace. Thomas' clipped bushes had stood out around the country house, trying to be beautiful, bristling prosaically.

She now took her pills methodically and went out to look at the roses in the garden. She decided to do some weeding. She had to do something. Five o'clock. The house was filled with clocks which chimed the hour, the half-hour, the quarter-hour.

Each time Thomas went off to town, she anxiously reviewed her failings. It would be different the next time. She would tell him that brown hair would suit him marvellously; she would flatter him, reach out for him — but here her promises stopped.

She had withdrawn from his embraces little by little, deliberately and cunningly, until the renunciation was complete. There had been his long stream of entreaties, the abasement, the marketing; then, a long period of silence in which she had smiled to herself. But while she had withdrawn herself from him, she had forgotten his hours at the office. For him, there was an escape; there were other people in the world besides herself. She suddenly feared that he would leave her. Her series of illnesses then began. Yes, her lamentations, her diseases, they were real enough and they worked.

Evelyn reclined on a lawn chair, recalling events. Thomas had given her a colour television set for Christmas, and they had laughed superficially over wine. Always, the gray sky that seemed to disintegrate into a thousand feathers, endlessly falling; and the television reminding her of world happenings. The first time that Thomas had walked in a little drunk . . . She always pretended not to notice.

The fountain gushed in the pool — a new installation this spring, Thomas' idea. The five o'clock chimes sounded. Far away, a doorbell rang. (But Thomas carried the house keys.) The doorbell again. This time she knew she was not dreaming. She walked across the patio and went around the corner of the house to peer suspiciously. A man stood ringing the bell impatiently. He was handsomely tanned, a streak of silver in his hair giving the lie to his youthful appearance. He looked ruffled and unkempt; he had driven up in a small foreign automobile.

She felt as if she had fallen from a building. Although some twenty years had passed she recognized him. She went towards him, tripping over some branches Thomas had clipped off and left.

"David! But where on earth do you come from? After all these years!"

He looked up, at once surprised and disappointed. She looked old.

"Evelyn, my God, it's good to see you again!"

He moved forward as if to embrace her, but checked himself. Nothing seemed very real. He knew he should say something, but he sensed the banality, the artificiality, into which their conversation would drop. Neither would admit the utter waste. Or had it been a waste for her? In the uneasy silence, he realized how foolish his sudden visit must seem.

"Evelyn – you're looking splendid. As fresh as ever! You haven't changed at all."

"Still the old flatterer, David. You haven't changed either."

He had been right about the conversation. It was wrong, all wrong. He was seized with the desire to run back, but knew he would have to bear through it. He could have slapped her for looking so composed. His misery was complete as they sat on the patio with drinks.

"You've got a beautiful place here."

"Yes, we're very proud of it, Thomas and I. My husband is so clever at keeping things looking neat and well. How do you like the fountain? It's the latest thing."

"Very nice. But where are the children? Or do you have any children?"

"No. No children. But we get along anyhow, you know."

She brushed her hair back and sat up, erect.

(The same gesture. The same embarrassment, he thought. She's married, and she still sits up rigidly, she still doesn't want to think about her body.)

"Do you have any children?" she asked him.

The pause was amost imperceptible, although he knew in a flash that he had to lie.

"Two children!" he replied, "a boy and a girl."

"Two! How lucky you are. They must be big by now." The shock rather hurt.

The fountain splashed in the five o'clock heat. The sound of ticking clocks came faintly from the white house. They avoided looking at each other. He felt miserable. His thoughts floated back to the war. That too seemed unreal here. He hated her ignorance. For her, it had been nothing more or less than a rumour. All at once his suffering and waiting seemed a ridiculous drama.

"I guess I've just been a hermit all these years," she said, "and Thomas – he's – why, he's just wonderful for me. Exactly what I need."

The six o'clock chimes began. Evelyn, jolted into the present, sat up erect. David dutifully glanced at his watch. Until he realized he wasn't wearing one.

"Oh," he mumbled. She looked at him and laughed.

"You don't have a watch on!" she exclaimed with glee.

The old guize was quickly resumed.

"Thomas should be back soon."

"I'm sorry I can't stay; I've a plane to catch. You'll give him my regards."

"You mean you can't stay for dinner?"

"Afraid not. But it was wonderful seeing you again. You look splendid!" he shouted, ducking into his car. She stood, puzzled and suddenly beautiful, on the steps.

That was how he would remember her. Like that. He started the motor.

"But wait!" she cried, "What's your address? When do we see each other again?"

"Sometime soon." he replied. "No. Never."

He drove off, feeling like an idiot, or worse still, like an adolescent in the throes of a first love.

She tried to reconstruct the short visit, but his image pushed all her thoughts aside. She sighed. She sat in the lawn chair until the clock sounded the half-hour, and she heard the familiar sound of Thomas' car in the driveway. He walked up the patio steps uneasily.

"Evelyn? Evelyn? Where are you?"

He saw her beside the pool. There were two glasses on the patio table.

"You don't usually have two," he remarked.

"No. This time I decided to have a fling."

"Have you taken your pills?"

"Yes. And did you find your papers?"

"Yes."

They walked together to the house, where she would begin dinner, and he would watch television. But this time, as he missed the last step and swung dizzily into the front door, she felt bolder.

"Why Thomas," she remarked, in a tone he had not heard before, "you're stumbling about as though you were drunk. What on earth did you do at the office?"

3. THE VOICE OF THE LOVER

FOR HIS FATHER'S SON

1.

Death in a country house:
throat convulsing, a dead man
the bed still warm
the trees he had planted growing
his paintings wet in a downstairs room

sunshine not warming him

2.

Convulsion in the heart
and a dead man
whose impassioned writing
I packed in boxes,

hiding his pain from you
as though it were mine,
guilty at the heart breaking
in his journals,

speaking to you, his son

3.

Death is objective.
Embarrassment, a fact for disposal.
I hid his writing
they cut down his trees
finished the undone harvest,

the axe chopping, chopping

           4.

His father's son
seven years to the day
grieves, grieves
leaves me, taking away

the last paintings
the final boxes
bonds to bring down heaven

My desolation, his,
whose mourning is greater?

CLAY

o fine-veined frozen leaf
lettuce in my brown bowl
o delicate white fibers

and veined my frozen heart
buried in beating clay
o final burial

TAKING LEAVE

So unaware, you cannot know
my grief as I listen
to our careful conversation
and sense the change in you,
your plans that fix
a thousand miles between us
though you sit, happy,
and for you the days darken
in painless waves, and we talk.

From another darkness, my mind,
mentor of what I can say,
prevents the wounds I could
inflict, makes me pleasant,
though I watch, amazed,
the gold sentinel who guards
your past, your present difference
under lock and key.

YOUR HEART

Your heart
has reached those outskirts
where snow blinds me
fences cross and blacken
my footsteps slacken in snowdrifts
far from our ecstasy

As any wanderer might,
this way and that, stumble upon
the right road, drunken —
wise for the right path, yet foolish
to know nothing of its rightness —
I in my maddened new geometry
turn circular in the whirlwind
left in your wake —
always your fool

In territories fenced from my approach
your heart beats stricken in hiding
a handful of embers against snow
gathering new flames from the wind:
while I cannot repeat
words we could never say
and talking to myself
leave you in dreaded silence
my face to the frost

ABSENCE I

not at night when darkness
draws away the gardens
and the horizon escapes my grasp
growing so much vaster

not shadows, not being alone

but setting forth, pressed on
by one who speaks of loving me
– the street crazily filled,
the traffic incongruous –

then the passing of these years
is senseless, and your absence
freshly absurd, strikes me down

ABSENCE II

I shall be almost casual about grief,
stroll down the crowded street smiling
or finger a child's toy without a sigh.

And I shall flee the bold challenge of your eyes.
That love was too much. I shall wander alone,
a stranger to my own madness.

Another world shall cradle my desperation:
trees without colour, swaying to no tears,
and faces, happy and intolerable as doom.

GYPSY'S REAPPRAISAL

Love has no power except love.
I'm no gypsy either, come to
ruin you with expectations,
prophesy and charms.

You weighed my advantages
as though they were knives,
already you cried out.
But all my advantage is love.

This is no power play.
Give up your words.

BITTERSWEET

1.

Pools of water, in
sunshine, might seem
still and sweet,
if not for rushing falls
on all the cool stones
making the moss bitter.

2.

We might languish here,
unthinking, making
pools for each other,
if not for those falls.
More than by reflections, we
are touched by bittersweet.

3.

I might grow bitter,
that night must take away
both pools and falls,
if not for bittersweet:
that I for drink shall
taste of all your mornings.

HIS GIFT
To Ted B.

You gave me perfume –
"White Witch" –
from an island of black sun
where you were travelling.

Is my spell, then,
vague as its essence,
cold at the back of the neck?

You gave me only
this witch's legend,
her three black husbands
hanging from palm trees.

MY GIFT

I thought I was in love.
The waters of your eyes
sparkled sunshine, children,
every blonde head bobbing
became my child and yours.

I swallowed moments
whole, a hungry mystic.
I didn't understand when
you didn't speak more clearly:
your smile seemed so clear.

Like water, you mirror the seasons,
you fashion a cult of yourself.
Now everything goes up in flames.
The autumn suits you, Ted
tomorrow you will be in cinders.

STARS

Laughing you phrased it, in
cool evenings: "censoring the
stars" – that clouds censor,
and stars vanish.
   (We are both
trafficers in loss, and calculate
depths; both theoreticians,
experts.)
   Listen: sometimes a star
crosses the evenings of your eyes,
and will not vanish.
   (Somewhere beneath
your breathing is my breathing, above
us, galaxies for exploration;
this beauty gathers, each
being-with-you easier in time,
each time;
   something within me
cancelling all thought; and only
feeling, as clusters of light,
curves to my body: endless,
this light-gathering.)
   Listen: no, I will not
censor those stars.

REROUTED

The world turned craftsman, and
all in a morning?
    This little
neighbourhood roars me into
awakening, all on a dawning
lazy my neighbours now pounding,
painting, rearranging.
    Calendars
overturned, that nice
fixity of habit: noise and
newness bursts upon me.
    (There was no point
to conversation save to reach
the inarticulate point: gestures
easy, hands without fear, the
voice not trembling. Wordy,
we strive for all this, all
at once silent to find it.)
    My quiet ways
wrecked, the demolition team
all in a row laughing, busy
my neighbourhood on a clear
morning:
    (I wake to all this, my
roots shaken by you and,
understood, rerouted.)

REQUIEM FOR PRISONS
I

Do not, holy One, leave me
your robes fluttering will
hurl me into a death
of lovers' arms

without you, I will not know
their love from His love
passion from Passion
I shall grow ugly, kissed

by too many. Priest, pray
for my one Embrace
even as you go,
even as you must go

REQUIEM FOR PRISONS
II

The child, in reverence
taped 2 popsicle sticks into a cross
took scissors to His picture, arms wide,
about to glue these together

heard another voice: "Haven't they
put Him up there often enough? "
and threw the miniature away
stunned by His blue eyes.

REQUIEM FOR PRISONS
III

To be the child
touching His white hem
bliss and the blue sky

not the disciples groaning
for a kingdom of crystal
for the final nightmare

To be the child of faith
without history, ignorant of
Hitler, the obliteration

REQUIEM FOR PRISONS
IV

Your repetitious love
makes you ugly;
who wants a love
so freely given?

It makes me feel
you have nothing to hold back,
nothing for yourself
for any others

each time you tell me
my soul shrinks
from the humility
of your obedience

It makes me wonder about
Our Lord
Who loved everyone always
and how He was hated

REQUIEM FOR PRISONS
V

I lie to you
so easily
moth
in a closet
you slip
into fabric
believing
believing

I deny you
you let me
let you down
so often
you stare back
like a goldfish
mute
mute

4. THE VOICE OF THE ABSURD

VOYAGES

This house in August,
in late August, is
unfit for life. Snow
comes over the river,
without prophecy. The
sudden cold is not
kept out by windows.
Noise turns inside
this house. Plans
to leave, to go elsewhere,
are made. Nobody
goes elsewhere. The August
wind leans inward with weight.
No walls have fallen. Plans
continue, imperatives
to go outside, to go
anywhere else. For a walk.
To the beach of stones.
To see a boat, a bird
in flight before winter.

Night
is never soon enough,
taking away whiteness,
too many highways
of white doom. The
blackness is never
thorough enough.

I file my nails down. And
they grow. This house grows,
distant from cities.

My life is out of my hands.
Others, below, devise routes
for my hands to follow.
Their voices
scatter me into
unknown voyages;
eyes like compasses
whirl and plot
the skeletal direction
of my fingers.

Never remain in a house
which is dangerous to the soul.

I hear and ignore
my own plea, its
urgency. There is
much talk. We
cannot decide to go,
so many calendars
prevent us. I have said
good-bye so often, with
packed suitcases, and
dreamed you would take me:

Into my own horror,
sleeping,
I have taken you.

My breathing becomes
someone else's moans,
less recognizable.
I am salt water, fetus,

avoiding light.
One hundred white leaves
hit the window;
this house
grasps and keeps us,
every one.

Occasional footsteps
on dirt road. Bats
follow the light, crazed
and utterly blinded.
In white
fall weather,
only my nightmare
screams.

THE RIVER

I gather stones and shells
the river swells at mid-tide
covering the rocks, no change
since I last walked these shores

the same faces peering from driftwood
the same arms yearning from boulders
reaching from some awful age
to pull me closer still to their stories

how many women blinded by the river
cursed by day-long family
joined hysterically with the river
to become a distant caller

men too tired gazing at ships
at some exploding sunset
fell and worshipped the slow passage
the tide the sails the water

now with their children's children
leering and drunken from the tide
caught forever in the myth of the river
their carved bodies singing from stone

I gather now as I gathered then
their knuckles and stone eyes
and read their history from my palms

their family is not beautiful
their past maddens the tides
and water closes over their faces

at high tide only, the river releases me
as the long dreams are over
I break these shells to pieces and recover

ELEGY

1.

We will remember
   a few rituals,
rain on the green leaf
   the whole ocean
      when the snail moves
rivulets of spring
   a few dewdrops
birds awakening
     songs of the marshes

We have philosophized
   on the four elements
brought values to birth
   recognized beauty
now, when we are still able
   to speak of delicacy

2.

   I see before me
scuttering, sly, rattling in and out
rulers of an empty wreckage,
   the cockroach

3.

It has no delicacy,
our devastation.

UNMARKED: AT LAUTERBRUNNEN

At the meeting-place
of two mountains, a valley,
carved by some glacier's
tooth, two waterfalls
that meet, mingling thier
opaque streams.

The mountains rise
over the valley:
clean stone shudders
in the height, and up there
bristles with evergreens until
a new height of edges
dissolves into snow and air.

Below, there is only
the valley: houses, ordinary
life, and man, dangerous
in his looking up.
A criss-crossed
graveyard, with marking-
stones upright like splinters,
and greater stones, unmarked,
that rise, and remember no one.

YOU'RE IN AGAIN

1.

You're in again, and this time you
need a comb. I think of the tiny
objects you try to gather. Last time
you needed dimes for the hospital
phone. I brought you sweet soaps
and honey and looked at your wrists.

2.

The other patients had
already become your friends, the
Polish woman who kept forgetting
her English and wouldn't
talk in the end, the tiny British lady
speaking of her sickness quietly.

3.

But you did not conceal your
hate in sweetness and quiet.
Your slashes cut across the room.
Your veins exploded in front of nurses.

4.

Their efforts to discharge you are futile.
You leave in anger, at your own pace,
and return holding the ticket in,
pills or razors or a knife, presented
at the door to confound all schedules.

5.

I go from honey to bittersweet,
assessing your need and my obligation.
I cancel visits from too much pain,
again scarred by your anger,
my own wrists aching with blood.

YOU RETURN

You return when I've
hurled you across continents
far into void: my safety perilous

(locking my doors against snow,
your eyes drawn to my lights
like claws in dreams or foxes
sniffing blood)

Your hunt is delicate, your
paws do not like snow,
hunter and pilgrim of heartbeat

My cabin faces north, naked,
snowdrifts melt with your step
a tiny trace of cruelty your path

you hurtle back
from absence, fox bewildered
pawing the snow in innocence

BONNIE & CLYDE

Like Bonnie & Clyde
at the end of the show
I'm face to face
with your deadline

All the hills of flowers
and the wide-brimmed hats
the gunshot adventure
and the slow motion kisses

My throat's cut through
the world's stopped
a second ago
you left my thighs

MICHAEL I
March 2, 1972

                "I suppose love, too,
                is a kind of frame
                for seeing a beauty
                that was always there."
                (from someone else's
                letter, the same day)

From Medicine Hat
at five in my afternoon
your voice on the phone

Isn't it strange –

                I pictured you still
                in your sloping room
                listless, with your books
                and irrelevant courses

– even when you said
where you were headed,
ties cut loose

                though in a month
                I could have seen you
                in your room in Toronto
                to talk, in between
                Cavett and Chinese food,
                not expecting any highs

From any hotel out west,
your pauses tighten like a rope
around my guts

I try to guess
when the pain will ease off

Breathing against telephone time
between Quebec and Alberta
we're close now, Michael
with this kind of last chance
to show our love

MICHAEL II: FOR THE TIME BEING

"I always have to work at holding on to myself.
There is a lot of destructive energy in the house.
Susie is going through what she calls 'a severe
identity crisis' and is suicidal at times. A tense
and difficult situation – but funny and pathetic to say,
for the time being it feels like home."
– January 4, 1975

Michael, I hope I am not
intruding, quoting your letter.
But you said there must be more to
life than putting in time, going
through the motions; some proof
against a simple suicide.

I have no simple proof,
not even human love.
'We're born astride a grave'.
I lie in it.
A man's body
urges me further down.

I look up
at the believing penis
– the old cock and balls story –
and sink ecstatic
to the earth: my glimpse
of death.

Though I'll age, I'll
live to see my hair
whiten, while stars

a couple of light or
dark years away
whirl unconscious from

Our bare bottoms
sperm and lips
our matter
feeling like home
for the time being

MICHAEL III: Susie, died 1975

1.

in living, common as so many
in death, by her own doing as so many
creating no especial precedent
simply removing from the world
    her only beauty

2.

does your last employer know
as you typed so well in downtown Toronto
or the man selling newspapers, Yonge & Bloor
or the people of India
    as you bartered
your life for some vision
your antiques for hash?

3.

Michael was waiting in love in Vancouver
your taxicab driver always stopping in time
your always student who quit each time
so young so old
    did he know
you had no reasons in particular
you had all the reasons in the world?

4.

Everyone promised
to get to know you
the next time around

It must have been
your sad resignation
the pools in your eyes

            5.

And before you jumped
was it crawling ants
or a sudden vision
awaited so long?

Pavement rushing
to meet you face-to-face
in life the coming down
was never so high, Susie

WHEEL OF FORTUNE

In the midst of grief
two fortune cookies
reading in sequence:

1. It will never be the same
2. It's best to laugh about it

SANITORIUM

Silenced in obscene pain
they lie, the cancerous and sick
down the corridors and halls
they breathe.

White rooms, each corner
grown familiar, each gray mark
fondled by closing eyes
white cells, suspension without reason.

Solid buildings, well hidden,
and solid trees. Inside, an arm stirs
with an intense defiance,
but green leaves outlast the gesture.

Flowers in gardens, showing their sexes,
the scent comes like a blow
the sick stare at their windows
clouds stare back without shame.

Pale wind at windows, drifting
into rooms of torment; pale sun
that blossoms on their walls,
terminates the argument.

ALCHEMY I

With you, only giving is left.
My empty hands touch you to receive
yet you transform my need as yours

Kisses taken from your mouth are given
your softness stolen resists my theft
you make it so

That beside you, to beg is impossible
your logic resists whatever calculation
I cannot quantify nor draw equations
nor try your loving with common divisors

Thus beside you, I must always give
though my intent may be to take away
so that my beggar's gold is endless

You make it so, you make it so

ALCHEMY II

When transformation so occurs
that hearts leap to desiring gold
and water, earth, air, separately
no longer satisfy

elemental division desires the whole
confusing all mathematics, creating
from clear separateness of emotions
new sorrow, desperation, love

when all before was cleanly divided
with definitions acceptable to mind,
hearts bound at magic irrational
love breaking all bounds

so that the human mind, magician not at all,
stares bewildered in double agony:
the new-found unity in bliss;
the golden sorrow, worse than any dream

LONGING

as fruit is perishable
so will I perish
forced from the tree
and so, without roots

as fruit decays
to smell of yeast and brandy
such sweet decay
so too my body

lifted, detached without reason
the apple swings its last in the air
without the bough's nurture
caught up in sudden whiteness

no part of what I see
but separate in consciousness
so too my mind swings
reels in a void

having understood nothing
neither world nor time
through self's separateness
my white agony

let me, as dim branches
desire the darker source,
return the futile self
to become Becoming

AUTOBIOGRAPHICAL NOTES

AUTOBIOGRAPHICAL NOTES

When I was a teenager growing up in Quebec City, other students used to ask me what personal quality I hoped to achieve in life. Some wanted charm, others intelligence, others generosity. Some time during my second year at Bishop's University in 1967 I came to the conclusion that what was most important for me was to achieve honesty. Now that I am three years from thirty, I realize the arrogance which this statement implies; nevertheless it is upon this arrogance and this quest that my poetry is built. One's personal life has a way of dragging its embarrassed behind and trying to catch up.

I lived in the Eastern Townships of Quebec for a while and have always regretted leaving. I promised to return, but sometimes returning means retracing one's footsteps, and life never really permits one to go backwards but pushes on, however painful that is at the time. Now I have an M.A. from Carleton University, and an editorial position with the federal government. The degree is meaningful to me only in so far as it allowed me to work under Dr. Adam Tarn, a drama critic, one of the few geniuses of our time, a man whom I dearly cherish. My editorial career is a continual exercise in self-discipline; at best it helps me to try to write well, and at other times it pays the rent.

I live in a highrise in Ottawa. My life style has often appalled those who knew me when I lived in the country, or who know me as a poet and carry a preconceived notion, usually of a mystical bent, of what that means.

I have published three books with Fiddlehead Press, won Canada Council grants and appeared in anthologies. It is difficult to be a poet, pay the rent, and love — but those are my life's necessities, though never in the same order.

I have been married and I have been single, and I am still trying to learn that what is important is not the outward form of my life, but the times that I am able to love.

I try also not to confuse the blunt honesty that sometimes illuminates my poetry and hopefully makes the moment worthwhile, with the on-going unravelling process which is my life and my confusion. I hardly claim to embody such honesty, though that ideal is my only star and I remain its most avid star-gazer.

Brenda Fleet
August, 1975
Ottawa